A Day in the Life Of

A Dandelion

Ruby Tuesday Books

Ruth Owen

Little Acorns

Published in 2025 by Ruby Tuesday Books Ltd.

Editor: Mark J. Sachner
Design: Tammy West
Production: John Lingham

Photo Credits:
Alamy: 20 (Joe Blossom); Dreamstime: 9 (Ruslan Galiullin), 19 (Luayana), 21 (Kateryna Chyzhevska), 22T (Msundfors), 23T (Lucian Coman); Nature Picture Library: 12 (Adrian Davies), 13 (Bence Mate); Ruby Tuesday Books: 4, 7, 8; Shutterstock: Cover (Quang Ho), 5 (O_Solara), 6 (LedyX), 10 (Lima_84), 11 (Barbora Polivkova), 14 (Bess Hamitii), 15 (Thilo Wagner), 16 (WCPW Photography), 17 (Serg Zastavkin), 18 (Petr Ganaj), 22C (Svetlana Zhukova), 22B (Midori Photography), 23C (irin-k), 23B (Lois GoBe), 24 (LedyX).

Library of Congress Control Number: 2024941195

Print (Hardback) ISBN 978-1-78856-495-3
Print (Paperback) ISBN 978-1-78856-496-0
ePub ISBN 978-1-78856-497-7

Published in Minneapolis, MN
Printed in the United States

www.rubytuesdaybooks.com

CONTENTS

Hello, Little Dandelion!

It's a special day for a little dandelion plant.

Its fluffy **seed heads** wait for the wind to blow.

Today, the little dandelion will make new plants!

The little dandelion grows in the grass in a backyard.

One week ago, the plant only had leaves.

A dandelion is named for its **jagged** leaves.

Years ago, people thought they looked like a lion's teeth.

Soon, fat **buds** grew from the little plant.

Each bud opened and became a yellow flower.

Most people didn't notice the little dandelion.

But it was getting ready to do a very important job.

The dandelion's flowers made sweet **nectar** and dusty, yellow **pollen**.

Nectar and pollen are food for bees and butterflies.

A dandelion's juicy flowers are food for many animals!

Some flowers did not get eaten.

They closed up and died, and seeds grew inside.

Then each closed-up flower opened and became a fluffy seed head.

Munch Munch Munch

A dandelion's seeds are food, too!

puff puff puff

Now the wind blows the seeds from the seed heads.

The seeds float in the air on their fluffy **parachutes**.

One by one

the seeds float to new growing places.

A raindrop **PLOPS** into a seed's parachute.

Just right for a tiny snail to take a drink!

Now, there's just one seed left.

An ant takes the seed to its nest for food.

This is a close-up picture of a dandelion seed.

The seed is tiny.

But inside the seed is
everything that's needed
to grow a new plant.

Now all that's left of the little dandelion plant are its leaves and stems.

The leaves become a juicy snack for a hungry pet turtle.

The little dandelion's special day is over.

But soon its seeds will become

new plants!

Glossary

bud
A new part of a plant that opens to become a leaf or flower.

jagged
Having rough, pointed edges.

nectar
A sweet, sugary liquid that's made by flowers. It is food for bees and other insects.

parachute
A covering that fills with air and allows another object to slowly float to the ground.

pollen
A colored dust that's made by flowers. It is food for insects and many other animals. Pollen helps flowers produce seeds.

seed head
A flower that has died and is now full of seeds.

Index